HELLO REAL WORLD!

To order additional copies, please contact us.
BookSurge, LLC
www.booksurge.com
1-866-308-6235
orders@booksurge.com

JENGYEE LIANG

HELLO REAL WORLD!

A Student's Approach to Great Internships, Co-ops, and Entry Level Positions

2005

For my first alumni mentor turned friend, Shirley Rivera, who encouraged me to write an essay about my internship experiences, and I turned it into a book!
For my career counselor, Linda Hernandez, who helped me shed positive light on some initially negative experiences.
For all my peers who looked to me for advice about the job hunt.
For my family:
…my mother who always presented the challenge to fundraise $5000 on my own to participate in a summer internship with a nonprofit pre-university and to find a summer internship or go to summer school for the summers thereafter. I, of course, chose work!
…my father who always shows his support and communicates that he is proud of me.
…my brothers—I'm glad we're still growing up together!

ACKNOWLEDGMENTS

On Content

Special thanks to Thomas de Uriarte for editing several drafts of my book and providing the employer's perspective (and Jesse Ante for connecting me with Tom). Thanks also to Shirley Rivera for her continual encouragement throughout the process and getting her interns on board too. In particular, thank you to Margaret Zahller for commenting on an initial draft of my work and suggesting other topics I could include in making it even more helpful to students. I also appreciate her intern's perspective. Thank you to Stephanie Campbell and Lee Schruben for being the only two people of the two dozen I sent my draft out to who responded with encouragement.

On Publishing

Thank you to my second alumni mentor, August Fern, who shared some helpful sites from her aunt-in-law. Thank you to Jane Hyun, author of Breaking the Bamboo Ceiling, for sharing how she went about publishing. Thanks also to author of Brag, Peggy Klaus, for putting me in touch with Jane. I would like to thank the editors at Writer's Market, Alice Pope in particular, for helping me understand the publishing process and answering my initial questions. Thanks to another mentor turned friend, Kate Kerrigan, who always checked on the progress of my book and asked her author friend about publishing. I am in deepest appreciation for my colleague, Mark Lacy, who shares a passion for writing and first planted the seed about self-publishing. I also should thank my brother, Ben Liang, who also encouraged me to look into self-publishing. Also, thank you to colleague, Aaron Ping, for asking his "Aunt Judy", Judith Stephens to share some of her experience with publishing. Finally, with regard to publishing, I must express appreciation for Ali Safavi, friend and author of a similar guide, but for MBA students, called Landing Your Dream Job: A student-to-student-approach to career development.

Ali inspired me by his self-publishing success. Thank you to Kelly-Ann Henry for connecting us! Thank you to Hugh Henry at BookSurge for the generous offer that sealed the deal and initiated my self-publishing adventure.

On Title Generation

I would like to thank Martin Wong, Shehzad Wadawala, and Ali Safavi for their contribution to the final title of my book. I also would like to thank this long list of people I surveyed during my two-month effort of title generation. I will exclude those mentioned elsewhere.

Albert Liang	Jeff Hong	Luyang Jiang
Alex Perwich	Jennifer Vorih	Mahesh Bhupalam
Allen Chang	Jerri Kay-Phillips	Michelle Davis
Andy and Melanie Reinersman	Joan Massola	Mike Goins
Anthony Yau	John Grams	Pete Hartigan
Cynthia Tsao	John Stiehler	Rachel Jackson
Dana Bolstad	Jon Burgstone	Ronald Ong
Esther Heller	Jonathan Sew Hoy	Seena Drapala
Franklin Davis	Joseph Yeh	Shaun Adams
Gina Rieger	Ken Susilo	Suzanne Jenniches
Graydon Hansen	Linda Sorauf	Tiffany Meier
Heather Hughes	Lisa Martin	

On Cover Design

I would like to thank Chi Vu for the cover design and Nan Jayaram for referring the graphic designer, Jona Hyun, while I was contemplating what to do with my cover. I'd like to thank my friends Allen Chang and Brandon Ooi who gave me their two cents on the final cover design. I appreciate my brother, Ben, the most for reminding me that one should not judge a book by its cover. With his tip in mind, I could go forward with a final decision knowing that some will like it, and others may not. However, the high quality of my book remains the same.

On Encouragement

I'd like to thank again Tom de Uriarte and Shirley Rivera as well as my friends at Cheers Toastmasters in Downtown Cincinnati.

On Marketing

Thank you to Martin Clayton for sharing tips from his self-publishing experience. Without Rose Adkins' writing workshop, I would not have met Maria Leon, who put me in touch with her brother Jerry Ross, who in turned shared Martin's name. Thanks to everyone caught in between too!

On Web Site

Lastly, I want to send a very big thanks to Brandon Ooi for designing my web site.

If I forgot to mention someone who contributed, please accept my sincerest apologies. That person gets a lunch and book on me.

TABLE OF CONTENTS

LETTER TO THE READER

Dear Reader,

This book is ideal for college students looking for their first professional job, whether it is a summer internship, co-op* (a term-long internship), or employment upon graduation.

Although the emphasis of my book is on getting a summer internship and thriving at your first job, the tips offered are applicable to any job search situation even if you've had a summer internship in the past and still don't feel seasoned for your next search.

I started this book while still a college student, and I understand how busy a student's life can be! So, I hope you will find this a short and refreshing read. Best wishes in your job search!

Sincerely,

Jengyee Liang

*APPPENDIX 1 discusses whether an internship or a co-op is more appropriate for you.

FOREWORD

"Two roads diverged in a wood, and I—
I took the one less traveled by,
And that has made all the difference."
—Robert Frost

When Jengyee reminded me that I offered to write this Foreword, less than one year had passed since our cathartic telephone call. I had encouraged her to write about her experience. As a result, Jengyee's insight for students and employers are expressed in this thoughtful and inspiring book about the internship experience (and beyond). She reminds others and me that work not only shapes one's career but also shapes one's life.

Jengyee and I met through the Student Alumni Mentorship Program at U.C. Berkeley. As an alumna, I wittingly knew that, when Jengyee chose me, I would have a captive audience for my college and career experience musings. Although our college majors differed, we expressed a similar passion about environmental issues. After several random talks about environmental-related careers, roommates, places to hang out in Berkeley, and dance places in San Francisco, our mentor-mentee talks quickly evolved into heartfelt conversations about enjoying life and making a difference in the world. It was during one conversation that Jengyee became my mentor—she inspired me to develop a formal summer internship program for my consulting practice.

What does Jengyee know about internships? She knows they can be fun, challenging, important, and well worth the experience beyond building a resume. She has completed three summer internships with well-known corporations. She offers a genuine perspective—the job search process, unspoken expectations, challenges, balancing college and work life, and positive and not-so-positive events. Most importantly, she understands how an intern (and employer!) can create a formative internship experience. Because of her core value to make a difference in the world, she is sharing her perspective in this book.

So for those who have chosen to learn from Jengyee's experience, I am assured that beyond building your resume, your internship experience can and will enhance not only your career path but other parts of your life.

Shirley F. Rivera
Founder & Owner
Resource Catalysts

December 2005

WHY I WROTE THIS BOOK

I am a recent college graduate (B.S. from the University of California at Berkeley in May 2005). I landed three paid, full-time internships at Fortune 100 companies (UPS, Merck, SBC Communications) during each summer of college even when the economy was shaky. I was disappointed by my first two summer experiences (primarily due to bad manager experiences) and even suffered from depression after my second one. However, after much reflection and conversations with my parents, alumni mentor, and career counselor, I learned to appreciate my abrasive first encounters with the professional world.

My third internship was very positive, and my manager's end-of-summer evaluation also reflected that. My manager rated my performance as exceeding expectations. Many of my peers have asked me for advice on landing and performing in summer internships. Thus, by popular demand, I led a workshop in January of 2003 for my peers on internships having completed only two internships at the time. In February 2005, I was invited to serve as a panelist for a student internship panel organized by my campus Career Center. I also advise my mentor turned friend, Shirley Rivera, who owns her own consulting practice and takes on interns, about how to structure an effective internship.

PART 1
WHERE TO START

CHAPTER 1
Reading Tips

For the Student

Students should read this book in its entirety including the appendix sections NOW. Reread each part as you go through each stage in the process and refer to the tips frequently. I also recommend reading Parts 5 and 6 prior to commencing and then again a few weeks or months into your new job.

For the Recent Graduate

If the "I need a job" bug just bit you, do not despair. You may be off to a slow start, but you have the luxury of time. If you're going to school or working, a big challenge is finding time and making the job hunt a priority. However, you don't need to worry about that. You can devote your full attention to finding a job. Note that if you lack work experience or if you've been unemployed for more than a few months, I suggest picking up a part-time job or volunteer work because employers like to see you make good use of your time even when jobless. Unless home is far away and you want to move back home and then get a job, try to stay on campus as long as possible so that you can take advantage of campus resources. My university career center offers alumni membership. Friends and professors usually are open to lending a helpful hand too. Stay connected. Pay particular attention to the sections on "try everything," "mingling," and "getting your foot in the door with externships." Good luck!

For Students About to Graduate

Although the focus of this book is on landing a summer internship or co-op, all aspects of this book are applicable to finding an entry-level position.

For Student Considering an Internship or a Co-op

In the Appendix section, I have included the pros and cons to doing an internship vs. a co-op. I would review this section first because it will play into how you plan your college career and how you approach each job search.

For the Employer

Recruiters and supervisors of interns, co-op students, and entry-level employees, you should understand that you play a large role in your employee's success. Work can be extremely stressful to those who are accustomed to the student life. You can put your new employee at ease by understanding his or her situation. This book gives you an inside look into a recent college student's first encounters with the real world. I encourage you to evaluate how you structure your internships and look for ways to improve it based on insights you gain from this book.

Although finding meaningful work for your new employee can be challenging, you should understand that this is important criterion that talented students will use to evaluate whether a company is right for them. If you truly are committed to recruiting and retaining top talent, please take care to provide a meaningful experience even if you cannot provide meaningful work.

What I mean by meaningful work is an assignment or multiple assignments that has impact on the business, is not tedious, and is well structured but allows some room for the intern to be creative or make decisions. The ideal project also would span across several disciplines or internal departments, which would give the intern an opportunity to interact with other individuals at your firm.

A meaningful experience in spite of a less than meaningful work assignment may involve several opportunities to conduct informational interviews with colleagues, to visit other facilities, tour a manufacturing facility or call center, or to attend training, special events, or panels on various topics. Whether the project assigned fits the bill or not, be sure that you explain to your employee the significance of his or her project to the business. If an intern or co-op feels that his or her time is wasted, that reflects poorly on the company. Parts 3-6 would be the most relevant for you.

For Everyone Else

Parents, mentors, professors, counselors, and anyone else who takes an interest in the success of the college student, you should draw parallels to your own job search and work experiences if a student asks for advice. Be encouraging and serve as a resource by offering to open up your network, critique a resume, or simply serve as a sounding board when the student encounters tough situations. Read the entire book including appendix sections once and take note of any passages that you find especially insightful for your student. Use this book as a reference.

CHAPTER 2
The Internship and Your Class Standing

Why Do an Internship or a Co-op

Experience is key to learning what you like and how to act in the real world. You've heard the advice about enjoying college and staying in school as long as possible because you have to work at least 40 hours a week for the next 40 years of your life. Some people will say this is reason not to work over your summers, but I would argue that this is more reason to gain experience sooner because the sooner you find out what you like, your work life will turn out much better. If you take the time to invest in your career today by doing an internship or co-op, you will greatly reduce the chances of getting stuck in a job you hate down the line.

Finding a full-time entry-level position is the real deal. You don't have the luxury of experimenting for two months and bailing if you end up not liking your work. So, you should take care to practice working and practice interviewing. Internships and co-ops are your dress rehearsals for your career. Once you enter the working world, you should plan to stay in a position at least two years, or your next potential employer may arrive at the conclusion that you jump ship at any sign of dissatisfaction. Although we are no longer expected to work with a company for a lifetime, companies still value loyalty.

Your Class Standing Dictates Which Actions You Should Take

Are you a freshman, sophomore, junior, fourth year senior planning to take five years? Don't let your class standing limit you. You can't be too early or too late. Indeed, the cliché is work experience is invaluable, and I'm afraid I must agree with that statement...three summer internships at Fortune 100 companies later! I started frequenting career fairs and company information sessions my freshman year.

A Note to Freshmen

During this exploratory phase, I didn't bother to dress up for these quasi-professional events. You can get away with sloppy campus wear and asking generic questions that indicate you have not done prior research on a company or position when you are a freshman. Enjoy it while it lasts. Review the "Art of Mingling" and "If All Else Fails, Go Work for Free". If you are intent on finding an internship the summer after your freshman year, do not fret. Just remember that finding a job is a number's game. The more you apply, the more you interview, the more likely you will end up with a job.

A Note to Sophomores

You should begin stepping up your game at this stage. You probably can get away with generic questions and not dressing professionally still, but you may not get very far depending on your field of study. More technical firms are open to business casual dress, and they may not prejudge you if you wear casual clothes to the fair, but why take that risk? I recommend you dress on the more formal side of business casual to be taken seriously. You will be a leg up above your peers when next year rolls around because having a summer internship before you graduate is almost a sure fire way to get you a job upon graduation. If you do an internship this year or simply participate in the job hunt process, you will be in great shape for landing one next year.

A Note to Students Planning to Graduate Next Year (and over Ambitious Sophomores)

Time to get serious. If you haven't been practicing, you may need to work twice as hard as those peers who were steadily building up their skills since their freshman year. Familiarize yourself with Part 2 of this book on the job hunt. Remember to be proactive, to try everything, and never to lose perspective that you may be just one interview away from hitting your magic number that will land you that offer.

Year in School	Target Position	Prior Experience?	Appropriate Action?	What You Can Get away with?
Freshman	Internship/ Co-op	Substitute work experience with campus activities where you demonstrate leadership. Focus on college, not high school.	Practice mingling. Consider working for free.	Questions without research, casual dress.
Sophomore	Internship/ Co-op	Substitute work experience with campus activities where you demonstrate leadership. High school does NOT count anymore.	Step up your game. I strongly encourage working this summer, or at the very least, start interviewing to gain comfort.	You still have some wiggle room with the questions and dress, but you should practice doing your homework on companies and being professional.
Junior/Year prior to Graduating Year	Internship/ Co-op	Work experience (even if unpaid or part-time) is key to differentiation.	Do your research and ask insightful questions to wow the recruiter.	Casual is likely okay for most technical firms, but play it safe and dress on the formal side of business casual.
Graduating Year	Entry-level Position	Work experience (even if unpaid or part-time) is key to differentiation.	Do your research and ask insightful questions to wow the recruiter.	Casual is likely okay for most technical firms, but play it safe and dress on the formal side of . business casual.

CHAPTER 3
The Internship Cycle and When to Start the Job Hunt

The Internship Cycle

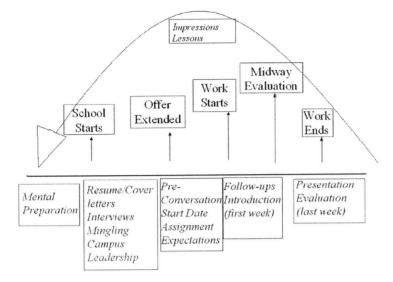

When to Start for an Internship?

You should start right now! I always started my job search in early September for opportunities the next summer. A handful of companies do their primary recruiting efforts in the fall, and they have a lineup of interns by December. Ford Motor Company and Merck & Company are two such examples. These companies tend to have well-structured internship programs. The majority of companies, however, like those that posted jobs at my campus, wait till February or so to begin interviewing candidates. Still, a handful of other companies wait till summer to determine their need. One of my friends managed to land a job during finals one summer and two weeks into his summer the following year. His luck goes to show that finding a summer internship once your summer starts is not impossible. I also had a similar experience one summer. I was two weeks into work at Merck when Applied Materials recovered from its hiring freeze and asked me if I were interested still. I was unavailable and relieved I did not wait on them. I favor the other extreme of searching nine-months in advance. You may not get your offer until April, but you are more seasoned than your peers in February and March if you begin preparing in October.

When to Start for a Co-op?

Since co-ops usually run for a semester-long (six months), I would recommend that you start a semester in advance unless sooner is possible. If you are on a quarter system, consider doing a co-op by taking off the spring or fall quarter and combine time with the summer vacation. Note that you have less "experimental" time for the co-op hunt. What I mean by experimental time is that you can practice the job hunt process during the fall semester or fall and winter quarters when you are looking for a summer internship. In a co-op situation, you have no clear experimental phase if you are on the semester system and only one quarter's worth in the fall if you are on the quarter system looking for a co-op for the spring.

When to Start for an Entry Level Position?

If you are planning to graduate in May or June, I recommend that you start your job search in the fall term. My friends who were serious about landing a job started in the fall and usually had received offers and made their decisions by December. This is a great position. Even if you do not land a job by December, you will be well groomed for the spring and should land a job with no problem by graduation time. The advantage to looking for a job while you are a student is that you can utilize all the resources available at your school's career placement office. If you are planning to graduate in December, you may be able to start your job search the prior spring. Otherwise, you are stuck with searching during the fall term if your intention is to start work soon after you graduate.

PART 2
THE JOB HUNT

CHAPTER 4
Keeping Your Mind in the Game

A Few Words About Me

I'm not the polished business student that always turns every interview into gold. I can be rather introverted. My parents were immigrants, so their circle of friends is a little limited. Translation: they couldn't hook me up with a job. In other words, if any of this sounds familiar, there's hope for you too. I landed three summer internships at Fortune 100 companies, including my first during the summer after my freshman year in 2002 when the economy was experiencing a serious downturn. If you're polished already, naturally extroverted, and born into a well-networked environment, by all means more power to you!

The Secret to Landing Any Job

Be proactive. Aspire to become polished, more extroverted, and well networked. Maintain your spirits high. Luckily, I'm inclined to be pretty optimistic, and I'm accustomed to working hard. I have several friends who graduated during the dotcom bust. Those who were proactive about their job search landed jobs in spite of the economy.

What Do I Mean By "Be Proactive"?

Being proactive is different depending on how far you are from graduating. If the light at the end of the tunnel is in sight, you need to step up your game. Freshmen, on the other hand, are in a great position to sharpen their skills and don't need to fret if they don't land a job during round one.

Being proactive basically means not limiting yourself to a single source for finding job leads. **Try everything.** If your family happens to be well connected, definitely approach your parents, relatives, and older siblings about job opportunities. However, as the saying goes, don't put all your eggs in one basket. Build your network. Seek out alumni mentors, visit your career center, frequent company events on campus, and attend conferences. Also, take advantage of any company events at the company. Intel had an open house day and invited a select number of students to participate in the tour. I was one of them, and I would have received an offer had I wanted to do a co-op there.

Opportunities often present themselves in the places you least expect, or they are disguised like the Intel Day. Actually, every job I landed had some element of luck to it. I found out about my first internship by an email sent to the alumni of a high school summer program a couple years after participation. A guest speaker from that program worked in human resources at the United Parcel Service in Southern California, and she posted an opening for internships on the email distribution. Although no positions were advertised in my field, I responded inquiring about opportunities in my field. I was aware that UPS was one of the few companies with a formal Industrial Engineering department, and I explained that this was my major. She identified an opportunity and setup an interview for me.

I found out about my second internship opportunity at a conference. As an officer of my university's chapter of Golden Key International Honour Society, I was fortunate to get subsidized for a trip to Atlanta on my summer vacation for the annual international conference. At the conference, I attended the career fair showcasing all of Golden Key's corporate sponsors. I had never heard of several of the companies until that weekend. Among the companies I did not know was Merck, the company I wound up working for the following summer. Although I did not hit it off particularly well with any of the Merck representatives at the conference, I remembered the name. As chance would have it, Merck visited my campus that September. I inquired the recruiter about internships and was encouraged to apply for a fellowship (an internship and a $5000 scholarship to assist in my academic endeavors). The application was due in November.

I found my third internship through my campus career center, but I was not completely dependent on my university's services. I was applying for internships through my campus career site, and I was landing a number of interviews. However, I missed the resume drop deadline for SBC Communications (now AT&T). I noticed that SBC was going to be a part of a career fair on campus the day before the scheduled interviews. Since I missed the resume drop deadline, I was not considered for the interviews. At the career fair, I approached the recruiter and asked if there were opportunities still available. The recruiter was impressed that I had done some research. After asking for my resume and questioning me further, he offered me a place on the interview list.

The job I accepted as my entry-level position also has a unique story. I initially really wanted to work for General Electric because I heard that it is one of the best places to start one's career. However, GE does not recruit on my campus. I contacted a Society of Women Engineers professional, whom I had met at a regional conference and whom I had kept in touch with over email, about forwarding my resume to the appropriate contact within the company. She gladly did so, and I was able to schedule an interview at the upcoming Society of Women Engineers national conference. I nailed the first interview and was invited to Cincinnati, OH for the on-site interview. While in Cincinnati, I decided to pay a visit to one of my professor's former students who works at Procter & Gamble.

My professor had mentioned his student to me a year prior, and I had noted he was in Cincinnati. My professor put me in touch with his student, and we setup a meeting. After a good chat with my professor's former student, he mentioned a few unadvertised openings in his current organization. I was invited back for a formal interview and received an offer. I did not receive an offer from GE. However, the culture at P&G turned out to be much more agreeable to me. I also had a challenging enough time narrowing down my other five offers to the P&G one without GE in that mix. I will discuss my other offers and how I arrived at choosing P&G later. For now, this just serves as another example of trying everything. Although all my other offers came from companies that recruited on campus, the best opportunity came from the one that did not.

Remember That It's Just a Number's Game

Along with trying everything and not limiting your search to a single source, you may need to try an approach multiple times before you get a hit. If you've ever done any fundraising (even selling girl scout cookies), you know that not everyone you ask will respond affirmatively to your request. Searching for a job is analogous. You are asking people or companies for something, which means you are bound to hear "No" many times. Here are some statistics for you: It took me only three interviews with different companies to land my first internship, and I had the same success rate my second time. However, I interviewed eight companies before I landed my third internship, and that was when I had two solid internships behind me. During my hunt for a full-time position, I ultimately received six offers after interviewing approximately

25 firms. I have friends whose interviews always result in an offer. Their success rate is 100%.

Your "**magic number**" (my term for the number of interviews you need to get your first offer per job hunt) might be three like my first-time at it, eight like my third time at it, or even more. Your magic number will be fewer if you're really lucky or really good, but also keep in mind this number changes each time you're on the hunt. You have no way of knowing your magic number until you get the job, so the trick is to keep perspective on the situation. I always have kept faith that there is a light at the end of the tunnel. If you are not as optimistic as I am, that is okay. Just don't let initial failures get the best of you. A job is waiting for you out there. You could be just one more interview away from an offer. Don't give up prematurely. Be proactive, try everything, and remember that it's a number's game.

Whether to Use Internship Placement Programs

Internship placement programs often charge a fee for use without the guarantee that you will land a job. I tried using INROADS (a program designed to help minorities land jobs) my freshman year, but I was turned off to it because I ultimately landed my job by my own means and did not care for the strings attached with INROADS membership. INROADS likely will open more opportunities to you, but make sure you read the fine print. Unless you are really good at convincing your adviser otherwise, you will be asked to return every summer to the same company and ultimately work full-time for your first company. If you do not mind continuing with one company, then this could be a really great program for you.

My other experience with placement programs was when I had my heart set on an international internship. The placement service I found charged nearly a grand just to apply. I was not willing to put up that money upfront and also abandoned the effort to find an international opportunity on my own. I decided I did not want to exert the extra energy developing and seeking out international resources, which I did not have.

CHAPTER 5
Don't Believe Everything They Say

Grades Are Secondary!

In general, companies are willing to interview students with a GPA of a 3.0 or higher. Some consideration is given to special circumstances (like if you financed your own education during college—you should say so if that's the case), or if you are an engineering student, or you go to a very difficult school. For some of the big name consulting firms, they want to see at least a 3.5 regardless of circumstance. You can try recalculating your GPA to include only the upper division classes applicable to your major. This is known as your "Major GPA". If it's higher than your overall GPA, you should list it alongside your overall GPA on your resume. If it's not, don't include it! Companies understand that you tend to shine in a subject that interests you (your major). Also, keep in mind that a perfect 4.0-GPA is not necessarily stronger than a 3.6 and balanced life. I fell into the second category. Lucky for me, companies value students who have social skills and other experiences beyond academics. They want to see if you will get along with your potential colleagues. Usually, if you make it to the interview, they know that you're smart. They just want to see how you will fit with the company and the position.

Additional note for those overly concerned about grades: be warned. The job hunt can be extremely time consuming and will cut into study time and sometimes interrupt class. Avoid classes where attendance plays heavily into your grade, or do your best to avoid scheduling interviews during that class. Take a lighter load if possible to free up your schedule.

The Grad School Debate

If you're wondering whether or not you should go straight to grad school or find a job, I'd recommend you choose one before going into your final year because applying to both can be overwhelming. I have friends who did both although I would argue that you couldn't do both and balance regular school on top of that very well. My friend ended up going to grad school because he didn't receive a job offer that he liked. If he were more focused on finding a job that he liked, perhaps things would be different. If you're set on going to graduate school though, you can apply straight out of undergrad when all the academics is fresh in your head. Some programs, especially business schools and law schools, highly encourage if not require work experience first. For higher technical degrees, work experience first is not a bad idea either unless you really know about what you are specifically passionate already. Working gives you a good sense of your likes and dislikes. Some companies even offer tuition reimbursement and will pay for you to return to school. The only challenge once you start working is finding the time to study for the entry exams, to apply to school, and to go back to school either part-time or full-time. I hear full-time is more effective, but that also means you're denying yourself a paycheck for a couple years. I personally went straight to work because I was burnt out academically and couldn't even consider the prospect of more school.

The Class Standing Paradox

If you are a freshman or a sophomore testing out the waters at a Career Fair, you might get shot down by a recruiter telling you that they only hire juniors. Don't let this stop you. A handful of companies will not discriminate based on your class standing. I had junior standing as a freshman, and I was not shy about telling companies so. I had junior standing because I entered college with over sixty units from attending community college classes and passing advanced placement exams during high school. Although the units did not count towards my major, I did benefit from the junior status when it came time for class enrollment and impressing employers. I am uncertain how much my junior standing helped, but it certainly didn't fail to spark interest.

If you wait till you are a junior to try again, recruiters will tell you that you lack work experience. So, if you don't land an internship, you better get a summer job regardless if you see a connection to the career you envision for yourself down the line. Some experience is better than none. Paid or unpaid, full-time or part-time, you should find work to get a flavor for working, and work enough so you can talk about it. See "IF All Else Fails, Go Work for Free."

CHAPTER 6
Finding the Opportunity

Visit Your Career Center Today

This step is especially important if you go to a large school. Get to know your career counselor by setting up an appointment with him or her to introduce yourself. If you go to a big school like I did, you need to be proactive here too in seeking out attention from your career services department. Explain to your counselor that you are looking for a job and would like to learn what resources the career services at your school provide to students. My university offers a free booklet that contains sample cover letters, resumes, and practice interview questions. The Career Center also offers free resume critiques, mock interviews, and e-newsletters on workshops on various career topics. However, you have to signup for all these services. Ask your career counselor or your well-versed friends how to signup so that you will be the first to know about mingling opportunities and job openings. The career counselor can be your best friend during your search process and even on the job. Sometimes, employers will ask career counselors to recommend students, so you should be sure that you are on his/her radar. My career counselor also came to my rescue after my disappointing second internship.

The Art of Mingling

I prefer the term mingling because networking has such a negative connotation, especially in the mind of students. You probably have friends who are naturals at it. For me, mingling was an acquired skill, and I still have not perfected it. I have practiced since my freshman year. Recruiters hate that you ask them ordinary questions, but you have to start somewhere. You can ask the recruiter what he or she does on a day-to-day basis and what kinds of job opportunities are available to you. As you step up your game, however, companies expect you to come prepared having done some research on the firm, the culture, and the advertised job opportunities. You are welcome to ask about opportunities that are not advertised, but they may direct you to another source within the company. I was able to get away with minimal research on the jobs posted because I had a good sense for what I wanted, and I could ask questions specific to the job that showed my interest. For instance, I knew I wanted a job that had more leadership dimensions to it than technical ones for my full-time work. So, I would ask questions like what balance of the work is technical vs. leadership? Or, what kind of training do you provide aside from the standard training program outlined on your web site.

With enough practice, you will develop the art of mingling, and expect to use it often. It will help you at a career fair, but you also need it during a comprehensive interview, where the company might take you to a happy hour. You also need to mingle well at conferences or alumni gatherings, which are great places to start building your own network. I've kept in touch with a couple people whom I met on a plane or at the airport. Mingling can be as simple or as hard as initiating a conversation with a stranger.

Although your intent may be to get a job, you should practice mingling for the sake of finding leads. You should be sensitive to others' willingness to help. Professionals who attend conferences and alumni gathering typically are very interested in helping students. However, people do not like to feel used. They prefer to help someone they know or a student who gives them a positive impression. So, do not ask them outright to give you a job. Getting the job is ultimately up to you, but people can point you in the right direction or push along the review of your application.

I enjoy making friends, so I mingle for that sake. This has served me well because I give my new contacts an opportunity to get to know me in follow-up conversations over email or at other events. Several of these new friends have invited me to apply to their companies without my asking about job openings. That's the power of mingling unleashed.

Attending Career Fairs to Warm up "Cold" Resumes

Cold calling is what telemarketers used to do; they would call complete strangers. This can be very uncomfortable for the initiator and the receiver of such a call because there is no established relationship or "warmth" between the two parties. A cold resume is one sent blindly to an employer. You are a stranger to the employer; you are anonymous unless you know someone who works at the firm who will put in a strong word on your behalf. A cold resume runs the risk of being disregarded just as you would deny a conversation to a stranger during a cold call.

Many have lost faith in the power of the Career Fair because most recruiters tell you to apply online. However, here are some reasons to attend a Career Fair.

- For some companies, this is a way to match the resume with a face. If you make a good impression here, the recruiter will put a star next to your name, and you are no longer in the stranger pile or cold category.

- You might run into your interviewer there, so you can make a good impression that will set the tone for your interview the next day or week.
- I missed the resume drop deadline for SBC Communications, the company I ended up working for as my third internship. I saw the recruiter at the Career Fair, and he signed me up for open spots on his interview day.

If you blindly submit your resume to an online system, it may well disappear into a "black hole." A Career Fair or Company Information Session gives you the opportunity to express to the recruiter that you are worried that your resume will get lost. Ask him or her if you can get the name and contact information of the person who will review the resume to follow-up on whether your resume has been reviewed. Then, send an email regarding your interest in the company to the appropriate person. If you did not meet the person at the Career Fair, this may be a cold email too, but your cold resume still stands a better chance of being reviewed. If possible, see if someone you met at the Fair can put in a word for you, or forward your email to the right person. Your contact will carry weight on your behalf.

Getting Your Foot in the Door with an Externship

Externships are one-day job shadowing events. Job shadowing is a great way to get your foot in the door. Ask your career center if an externship program is available to you. My career center paired underclassmen students with alumni over winter break. The Society of Women Engineers chapter on campus also ran a job-shadowing program for members over spring break. If you do not find a "matchmaker" on campus, you can create your own opportunities. Ask a neighbor or someone you met that has an interesting job if you can observe him or her for a day. The catch is that you find a day that is good for the professional and find a way to get to his or her workplace. On the day of the event, be engaged. Come prepared with some questions, and don't be afraid to ask too many questions that show you are interested in what your host does and about the firm itself. When you get home or the next day, do not forget to thank your contact for setting up an informative day for you. If you impress the people you met with your energy and inquisitive mind, they may ask you back for a formal interview.

CHAPTER 7
The 4-Unit Process: Treat This Like a Class!

If you take the job hunt seriously, you can expect to put in some long hours. Many of my peers would agree that the search for an entry-level position (and often that junior-year internship) is more time-consuming than a four-unit class. The job hunt is a lot like school in many respects. You need to do your research on companies and prepare for your interactions with company representatives. You need to do your homework in preparing your resume and studying for your interviews. Plan to spend several hours each week researching companies, doing homework, and studying. Instead of working towards that grade, you are working towards an offer. You can win bonus points by writing professionally and impressing professionals with your respectful persistence and charm.

Choosing the Right Company

What companies to apply to is a factor of what subject you are concentrating in school, what you want to do for a career, and where you want to be located. You should do your research on what industries excite you. What is most important to you? The position? The company? The location? Another factor?

Big Companies vs. Small Companies

I personally preferred big companies for my summer internships because I like a structured program. There are several advantages to big companies but also some rather frustrating aspects. I will offer some of my impressions of big and small companies, but these are generalizations. You should evaluate each company on its own merits because you may have some big companies that run as if they were small or vice versa.

Big Company Advantages

Big companies tend to have a lot of clout and can be more selective in their hiring because they receive so many applicants and have strict policies, such as requiring you to pass a drug test. Smaller companies look to them as leaders. So, if you decide to switch companies later on, that big name under your belt will not go unnoticed. Think of big companies like a popular brand. Why do you prefer a name brand to a private label? The quality of the product may not be much different, but you trust the name brand more. When it comes to work, big companies also have more resources and the infrastructure to help you. An internship-specific advantage to some big companies is that they have a huge internship program. One summer, I felt that I had a particularly lousy work experience. However, I was lucky to have made a lot of friends in the form of other interns that summer, which helped make me feel that my time there was worthwhile.

Big Company Disadvantages

Big companies tend to have a lot of bureaucracy. Just submitting my application or asking a seemingly simple question about relocation sent me in circles. The person who was supposed to be my primary contact turned out to be the wrong person. To make matters worse, sometimes this person does not even know who the right person is to address your needs, so your paperwork or questions remain stagnant. What seems like a very simple process can take much longer than it should, and you are required to be very patient and persistent throughout the process. Having a sense of humor is helpful. I had a situation where I accepted my job in December and consented that a background check be run on me. When I called my contact in April to inquire about my start date, my contact said I had not been hired yet because my background check was missing. She requested that I send in the consent form and copied my future boss. Luckily, I had saved the original email from December and explained that I did do so. She later found my form in the system archives.

Small Company Advantages

Many people prefer mid-size and small companies because the culture tends to be more entrepreneurial and much less bureaucratic. Concerning internships, small companies may take more care in making sure you have a worthwhile experience. However, they also may have very little experience in sponsoring summer interns, so you may experience some growing pains as they experiment with your presence. In this latter case, you should be very familiar with the contents of this book to help you make the most out of the experience. For instance, be sure to ask for an end-of-summer presentation and performance assessments.

Small Company Disadvantages

In addition to some small companies' lacking the internship

experience, they do not have that brand name appeal of a large firm when you decide to switch companies. They also have fewer resources.

Geographic Considerations

Much of my learning has come from being out of my comfort zone. Although I am not always in the mood to put myself outside of my comfort zone, I do try to put myself out there frequently. I would encourage you to do the same. The most growth I have experienced has been away from home, so I have accepted an out-of-state offer when presented with one. The different geography is fun to experience and tests your independence and maturity, which can help you feel more at ease when you encounter the "real world" for the first-time. One summer, I worked for Merck in a suburb of Philadelphia called West Point, PA (not to be confused with West Point, NY). I enjoyed living on the East Coast for the first time and being exposed to another part of our big country. Even though that work experience turned out to be a disappointment, I finally visited New York and Philadelphia for the first time and visited Washington, DC—one of my favorite cities—several times again.

Another dimension to geography is if you prefer a suburban or urban setting. Since I never had a car, my ideal environment is an urban one where public transit is available. However, most of my jobs have been in more suburban environments. In my out of state internship, Merck set up carpool vans between the residence and work place. Thus, I did not have to worry too much about getting around, except on weekends when I relied on other interns. You may want to clarify what a suburban environment means as well because my out-of-state environment was advertised as suburban but actually seemed rather rural.

Preparing the Resume

Sometimes, you can charm your way into getting an interview if you express genuine interest in a job to the right person. The more common route, however, is to submit a resume. Think about what you have to offer. Companies like to see work experience. If you don't have any, then you should list on your resume any activities where you've held a good degree of responsibility. Examples include volunteer work, campus involvement via an elected position in a student group or student government or dorm association, part-time jobs, any entrepreneurial attempts (founding a club on campus), planning a big event, organizing your own trip abroad. Some students like to fill the space with "relevant course work". I am not a big proponent of this because most work is not like academics. Instead, I listed my technical and foreign language skills. Computer literacy is pretty much a pre-requisite these days. It may seem commonplace, but you should list it.

You should have a polished resume that is easy on the eyes. Take care to format it so that you get strong marks on the presentation even if your content is solid. Go see your career counselor or call on alumni and other professional friends for a critique. I went through at least a dozen iterations to perfect my resume. If you make several versions of your resume, you need to polish every one of them. I have friends who applied across several industries, and they had a resume tailored specifically for the investment banking firms, another one for the consulting industry, and yet another general one for engineering positions. I was able to get away with just one, but I customized my cover letters. A cover letter is often optional but recommended and sometimes required. It is meant to grab the attention of the recruiter, so that s/he will look at your resume and consider you for an interview. If you are willing to devote the time, you should customize every resume and cover letter to each company for which you submit an application. Be sure you do not submit a letter to Company XYZ with your interest in Company ABC written all over it. That's a quick way to get your resume thrown out of the review.

Securing References

Most companies will ask you to provide three references on your job application. Do not overlook this step because companies do check your references! If an employer is interested, the recruiter will call your references to confirm that you are a strong candidate or to help break a tie between you and another applicant. When you list a reference, make sure that your reference holds you in high regard and will speak well on your behalf. Call the reference in advance for permission to list him or her as a reference. Ask him or her if you should provide any information, so that s/he would be more prepared when an employer calls about you. This offering of information about you is especially important when you ask a professor to serve as your reference because s/he may be familiar with only your academic performance and not your leadership capabilities outside of the classroom.

I often listed one professor and two contacts (often, students) from my extra-curricular activities. Most organizations have some kind of hierarchy. I listed the president of a student group as my reference. He was familiar with my accomplishments as an officer under him and was so happy with my work that he encouraged me to run for president as his successor. I used him as a reference even a year after I served as president of this organization. For my third reference, I enlisted another friend and graduate student, who chaired the volunteer committee on which I served by helping organize an event that brought together students and alumni. I similarly served as a reference for my friend, who served as vice president under me in another student organization. The employer who called about my friend asked me a few short questions about his character. She asked how I knew him, what were his greatest strengths, what motivates him, and what else I wanted to share.

If you have previous working experiences, you may consider using your former supervisor or other colleagues as your job reference. I never felt very comfortable doing so, but you may feel differently.

Preparing for Interviews

The number one tip on nailing an interview is to be confident and energetic while being yourself. If you are shy, you need to put yourself out there and be more animated. This is still you in content; you are simply altering the presentation to make it more interesting to the employer. Also, prepare a few stories on your team experiences, dealing with difficult people, and your strengths and weaknesses. Share only stories that are positive. Familiarize yourself with behavioral interviewing. Use the STAR method of narrating your story, and keep it concise without leaving out the details. STAR stands for situation, task, action, and result. If you prefer, CAR is circumstance/context, action, and result. What was the situation or problem? What did you do? What was the outcome as a result of your efforts? Use "I" vs. "we". You should recognize that you worked with others to complete a task if that applies, but make sure you communicate how you contributed to the success of a project.

Low Budget Phone Screenings

I was born and raised in California, so I was itching to try something new by my sophomore year in college. I really wanted to land a summer internship out of state, and I was lucky enough to do just that. If you are open to moving around too, you probably will encounter a phone interview. Companies probably are not willing to fly you out for an internship interview, so they will screen you on the phone instead. Phone interviews are nothing to be feared, and I actually preferred them because you do not need to worry about how you look and making eye contact, etc. I prepared for them by reading about phone interviews online. The two or three key things are to maintain good posture, smile as you talk, and raise your eyebrows to help the inflection of your voice. These tips may sound hokey, but the receiver places a lot of weight on how you sound because the other nonverbal cues are eliminated from this type of interview.

On Persistence and Follow-up

Follow-up religiously. Your first priority is finding a job, but your future employer has other work on his/her plate. Filling that summer internship position more than likely doesn't top the list. You need to call him or her to find out what your status is and what you can do to move it along. I recommend emailing and leaving a voicemail every other week. The phone call is important to direct the attention to the email you send because your email may get lost easily. Some professionals receive nearly a hundred or more emails per day. The voicemail is a way for you to get heard without impeding on the professional's busy schedule. Why email in addition to the voicemail? Email is a good way to showoff your writing skills and also reflects your respect of the employer's time. He or she has the option to jot a quick note to you in a few seconds rather than take the few minutes to return your call.

Be Professional, Especially In Writing

Take care to write a good email. An email is another opportunity to highlight your talents. Keep it short. Be respectful of other people's time. Professionals are busy people, and they will not tolerate long emails. Email within 24 hours of meeting that person. Offer pleasantries and thank them for their time in a line or two, and highlight a couple points from your interaction that are unique and would help them remember you. Finally, suggest further action or mention how you look forward to hearing from them again. Do not expect professionals to return your call. You need to do the follow-up. Do not write anything in the email that can be interpreted as a command. Read your note aloud or to a friend if you are uncertain how it sounds because you should know your place. At this stage in the job hunt process, you are at the bottom of the food chain. That's just how it goes, but you will impress by showing mastery of your terrain.

If All Else Fails, Go Work for Free

Work trumps not working. Work for your parent's or neighbor's company if you don't find an internship by your own devices. Or, volunteer for a nonprofit or ask one of the companies that turned you down if you can work for them for free. I cannot emphasize enough that working is invaluable, and you should appreciate that as an intern, you won't be stuck in your position for more than the summer if you're not enjoying yourself. Working gives you the opportunity to interact with people with different personalities. You are exposed to only a few personalities at school, and you can ignore peers that you don't like. However, if you come across a personality you don't like at work, you can't ignore your colleague. In my unfortunate situation, I couldn't avoid my boss either, but I learned what precautions to take the next time around to make my internship meaningful to me. Whether you think so or not by the end of your internship, you are better off for the work experience. If it was boring and seemingly meaningless, you probably gained from it in some respect. For instance, did you try anything to make it more interesting? Did you ask for more work? Did you befriend a colleague? Did you devise your own project? What was the result? Did you socialize with the other interns? Did you participate in company activities? Which of your strategies worked and which didn't? How did your boss react?

PART 3
FROM OFFER TO FIRST DAY ON THE JOB:
SEALING THE DEAL

CHAPTER 8
Offers in Hand—Now What?

Exploding Offers

I received several exploding offers, where I was given two days to decide whether or not I wanted the job. This probably means they really like you, but they have people on the waitlist. So, you need to act quickly. You may be able to request a few more days to make the decision, but they typically won't grant you more than a week. If this is your only offer and you like the offer, you should take it. If you turn it down, you don't know what the future holds. You may end up empty handed if you don't open the door when opportunity knocks. Note that I would recommend highly declining the offer if it's for an entry-level position because you don't want to go into that job feeling lukewarm. Unless your opportunity is rather exceptional, the company should give you at least several weeks to make your decision. You have much less wiggle room for an internship or co-op, but your objective there is to gain experience. So, do jump at that opportunity.

Compensation and Negotiation

I would not worry too much about your compensation, especially if it is your first job. Most companies pay pretty competitively, and you will make around three times the minimum wage. I never negotiated any of my summer internship offers. I had a friend that tried, but nothing came of it. I will not discourage you from trying because you may regret it if you don't. Unfortunately, I am not equipped with the tips for this.

Multiple offers? Lucky you!

If you have several offers in hand, you may want to negotiate to help break a tie. However, more than likely, one offer will stand out above the others. You should list what factors are important to you (the name of the company, the location, the culture, the people you met, etc). Then, rank the companies according to your personal criteria and see which one rises to the top. You can feel out the better option as well by going with your gut, which is generally recommended. I personally favored going with opportunities that put me out of my comfort zone, and I made myself geographically open to try new opportunities. If you are very close with local friends and family, you may choose to stay closer to home. However, don't be afraid to make new friends in a new place either.

Narrowing down My Six Entry-Level Offers

I effectively received offers from Danaher, IBM Consulting, Intuit, Procter & Gamble, SBC Communications, and Wells Fargo. I say "effectively" because I technically did not receive the actual papers from Danaher. They were trying to identify where to place me before extending a formal offer, but they were out of the running due to poor timing. I received a call from who I think would have been my boss the day I received my last formal offer and had narrowed down my offers to that last one and another one.

I initially had my heart set on a rotational program, where you sample typically four (three in the case of SBC) different roles, each for typically six-months (more like ten-months for two of the three SBC rotations). I basically saw them as four more extended summer internships (or four co-ops) clumped together. Danaher, Intuit, SBC, and Wells Fargo all offered rotational programs. Each had a different focus and a different flavor. Of them, Intuit's appealed to me the most because it had a rotation on process excellence, which was very much in line with the industrial engineering I studied in school and furthermore was modeled after the General Electric rotation I had pursued. It also had a marketing rotation, which sounded fun and different from what I studied. SBC came in as a close second because I loved my previous summer there, and the program is really unique in giving you hands-on leadership experience fresh out of school by letting you supervise people in the two 10-month rotations. I ruled out Danaher because of its purely engineering and manufacturing focus. I preferred the breadth of the other positions, and I wanted more of a leadership dimension in my career. I ruled out Wells Fargo because its program was just one-year vs. two. That seemed too fast.

IBM Consulting was in a category by itself. I decided to pass on the busy, consulting lifestyle characterized by heavy travel. The P&G opportunity also was in a category all by itself. It sparked my interest on several levels. First, it was a direct application of my major of industrial engineering & operations research. I had no intention of going into work involving engineering, but this opportunity made me reconsider. Second, both internal and external sources told me that working at P&G is like earning your master degree (for me, it would be a master of science in what I studied during undergrad and a master in business administration). Third, the job itself involved projects that would translate to big savings for the company. It sounded like I would be given a great deal of responsibility upfront and would get to contribute right away. With the rotation programs, I would have to wait at least two years (perhaps longer) before I was in that position of responsibility.

Next, the geographical factor came into play. P&G is in Cincinnati; the Intuit and SBC offers were both based in Northern California. For SBC, I was planning to request a rotation in Texas, where the headquarters is located. I had fallen in love with Northern California, but I also saw a lot of value to living out-of-state. I felt like if I stayed in Northern California, I would feel like I was settling down and ready to start a family. I was getting too comfortable, and Cincinnati would offer the discomfort factor. I'd be forced out of my comfort zone and would have to start fresh. A challenge I welcomed.

Saying good-bye to Intuit was not easy. SBC was my first love, and then Intuit came along. Even a year after I decided to forgo the rotational track, rotation programs still sound like fun. However, two items ultimately broke the tie for me. 1) The harder thing to do seemed like the better thing to do, and the harder decision to accept was P&G. 2) P&G had some perks. I would be allowed to attend some conferences on the company's dime. That was a huge big company advantage, especially since I love mingling and going to conferences! Of course, not every big company will sponsor such trips, but it was reassuring that the idea was far from foreign at P&G.

The tie breaking took a good two weeks spanning the week prior to and during final exams, but it was a necessary exercise. My parents were a great sport by entertaining my flip-flopping decisions. Monday, I woke up convinced I'd be accepting the Intuit offer. By Tuesday, I had changed my mind again. After some dialogue with both companies and clarifying what I could expect, I finally made up my mind.

Why Burden Yourself with Landing Multiple Offers

Here are a few reasons:

1) I find interviewing a lot of fun, and I've met several friends on interviews too. Is it unfair for the company or companies you deny? I don't think so. During the interview, you learn about the job. Once you receive the offer and compare it with others, you learn even more. Perhaps, the comparison even prompts further discussion with the company, at which time you again

learn more about the job. Until you know enough about the job to make a fair assessment of whether it's for you, you should not stop short of the offer. Money is usually an important criterion although it is not the most important factor for me. Especially if money is your number one item, you must get the offer in order to find out the pay.

2) Multiple offers force you to make an informed decision. You need to consider what's important to you in the process.

3) You should be aware of what else is out there.

4) Getting several offers is a good indication that you have mastered the art of the job hunt.

5) You should know what you are worth. A friend of mine with a chemical engineering background from UC Berkeley took the first offer that came to him. He later found out that he was being way underpaid. I made more than him as an intern at SBC than he did as an entry-level person at a small biotech firm.

6) Multiple offers also puts you in a good position to negotiate should you decide to do so.

CHAPTER 9
Preparing for a Smooth Transition

First Big Decision—Start Date

If you have flexibility in determining your start date, consider asking these questions: Will there be other interns? When are their start dates? You should try to synchronize start dates with the other interns or start prior to them. Some schools get let out especially early, so you may have little control over coordinating with the other interns. If you end up starting later than them, talk with your boss about what projects you can expect and get to know others right away when you get there.

Beware: Do think twice about when you plan a vacation! I went on a family vacation prior to the start of my first summer internship. If I hadn't traveled, I would have started work on the same day as most of the other interns. They were received with a formal orientation and introduction to everyone and greeted with the projects that were described to me. When I arrived, I had no formal welcome, except for a less exciting project than those that initially caught my interest about the internship.

The lesson that I learned from this situation was that I should have asked for a commitment from my boss that I would get the project described to me even if I went on vacation. At the time, I also was not proactive enough to make friends with everyone in the department on my own. Now, I would know better and introduce myself to new people if my boss did not do a good job at making the rounds.

Note that you should be aware of how much wiggle room you have in going on vacation that summer. Employers want to get as much time out of you as possible, and they may not appreciate your taking time away even if they grant you permission. Some employers will not even consider you for the job unless they are sure to get a time commitment from you, while others have official start dates. The reasons for these policies are that it takes a lot of effort to setup an internship and there is a period of "handholding" before you are able to perform on your own. If you shorten the internship by too much, your employer will be annoyed that they spent the bulk of the time just helping you feel comfortable.

Internship Program Structure

If you were hired into a formal program, chances are you will be working with a couple hundred other interns, and you will have several intern events lined up for you throughout the summer. You should clear with your boss before you start work or during the first week if he or she would mind if you attended these events during work hours granted you meet the deadlines for your work. I would encourage you to participate actively in the intern events. My second internship was on the East Coast. Though I wasn't pleased with my work experience, I made several good friends whom I visit on occasion. The other interns made my summer more pleasurable than if I had gone it alone.

The Pre-Conversation

Your search may be over once you've accepted the job, but your work has just begun. Find out to whom you will be reporting. You should talk with your manager-to-be before you accept a position if you have more than one offer. If you just have that one offer, you should take it, but make sure you contact your boss before your first day at work. Ask him or her about his or her managerial style (structured or more laidback). Does he or she have an open door policy if you have questions? Has he or she dealt with interns in the past? Will you be assigned a big buddy? If not and you want one, ask your boss for one. Are there intramural sports? What does your department do for fun? My department at Merck did a Habitat for Humanity project for a day as a team building activity. It was one of the more memorable days of my internship.

What will you be working on over the summer? If they say, "We'll wait till you get here", explain that it is important to you that you have a sense of what you will be doing before you get there. Explain that you want to do good work for them, and you need to be aware of what is expected of you upfront. At all times, however, don't be too demanding. Your conversations with your boss before you start work will set the tone of future dialogue. You want to be polite and diplomatic in what you say while getting the information you need and the projects you want. If you know what kind of project you want to work on, you can request to be put on a project in a specific area or get exposure to a particular area of interest.

Most of my peers never bothered with the pre-conversation. Indeed, I did not either during my first two internships, but I learned by the third time. I was disappointed by my mediocre reviews at the end of the summer. I had worked very hard all summer and strongly believed that I contributed high quality work. However, my evaluations did not reflect this. Perhaps, my managers were right and I should have done better, or perhaps they had other issues. Regardless of their motivation for giving me just an okay review, I did not want to get burned again. That is why, you should make sure that you and your evaluator are clear on what the expectations are for you from the get go. Sometimes, when you are applying for jobs, potential employers will ask for references from your previous employer. You are in a strong position if you are confident that your old boss will put in a good word on your behalf. Still other times, for reasons outside of your control, you may not get a strong review. In this case, refer to the section on "What to Do If You Left on Not So Good Terms".

What to Request

To reap the most learning out of your summer experience, you should have an end of summer presentation and performance appraisal. I would recommend a midterm appraisal as well. Most structured internships usually ask you to make a presentation on your summer project, but you should request one if they don't have one setup for you. I offer tips on making a presentation in the Appendix. A performance appraisal keeps you in check. It tells you whether your boss perceives your work the same way you perceive your work. A midsummer appraisal lets you gauge how you are doing and gives you the opportunity to improve on any weak areas so that the final appraisal doesn't come as a shock. My second manager talked me out of doing the optional midsummer evaluation because she didn't get a project to me until a month into my internship. We had scheduled the evaluation a week later. What I wish I had done was to request a three-quarters evaluation because I found the evaluation that ultimately arrived rather unreasonable.

Caution If You Come from a Prestigious University

Unless you landed a position with a company local to your school or a prestigious consulting or investment-banking firm, do not expect to find many fellow alumni. Most companies fill their job openings with candidates from local schools, which likely are not as highly ranked as yours. You should take care not to let your "good schooling" go to your head. Just like you don't need perfect grades, you don't need to attend a prestigious school in order to enter the workforce and succeed in the real world. Your employer is concerned with the work that you do, not your academic background. You'll make more friends too if you don't flaunt a superiority complex.

PART 4
ONCE YOU ARE THERE: SHINING AT YOUR NEW JOB

CHAPTER 10
What to Expect

Week One

During your first week one on the job, follow up with your boss on pre-conversation discussions. Get your expectations, go over them with your boss, and make sure both of you arrive at the same understanding.

Find out if your boss is laid back and open to your inquiries as they arise. Otherwise, setup weekly or biweekly sessions with your boss as a time to check-in with your boss. If you prefer a more casual setting, you might ask for a weekly lunch with him or her. The objective of these meetings are to make sure you are getting what you need out of your summer, and he or she gets the opportunity to learn more about you and lighten his/her work load by delegating some of it to you. Companies hire interns to test if they will be a good fit to fill positions on a more permanent, full-time basis.

Finally, introduce yourself to the others in your department. Your boss or buddy should take you around the department. If he or she doesn't, be prepared to go around and introduce yourself. If you are shy, you need to put yourself out there, and do it anyway. Your project may involve your colleagues or computer software unfamiliar to you but familiar to your colleagues. Know your resources, so you have someone to call if you ever need help. Just as in mingling, people naturally prefer to help people that they know. Your new colleagues most likely will not deny you help, but they may be more willing to help you if you make a good first impression on them.

Basic Protocol

Dressing for Success

You might need to invest in a new wardrobe. Business casual can be a rather ambiguous dress code. I always felt that I dressed more casually than my colleagues. Nobody called me on inappropriate dress, but I believe in feeling comfortable at your workplace. So, I began investing in more professional wear so that I felt more in line with how my colleagues dressed.

Punctuality

If you are salaried, you may not need to punch the clock. If your manager does not micromanage, he or she most likely will not be concerned with the exact time you arrive at work as long as it is reasonably on-time and you finish your work. However, I would advocate being on time to be on the safe side.

Time Management

You should exercise good time management at work. You do not have short-term assignments like in school that keep you on track. Rather, you have larger assignments and sometimes with no hard deadlines. Do what works for you. Lists help keep me focused on the task and intermediates tasks at hand. I also set due dates for myself sometimes.

Electronic Courtesy

Return voicemails and reply emails.

CHAPTER 11
Mingling at Work

Your Work Behavior: Workhorse vs. Social Butterfly

You are at work for eight hours. That does not mean you must be working for those eight hours straight. Although you go to school to learn, that does not mean it is actually in your best interest to get a 4.0 GPA. Companies value a well-rounded student and a well-rounded employee. They want to see you interact with your coworkers and enjoy yourself at work. I was really serious at my first couple internships, and I would work all the time and shut myself off from the chatterboxes in the cubicles near mine. I have not mastered balancing work and socializing at work, but it is an important practice. I tend to think that erring on the side of working too much is better than erring on the side of socializing too much. However, if you get your work done and done well, your boss and your peers will appreciate your spreading good cheer around the office. Don't take yourself too seriously. Avoid being a workhorse or a social butterfly.

Informational Interviewing

Is your work not very interesting and not keeping you busy? You might poke around other departments to see what the people who work elsewhere do. Ask your boss to setup half to one-hour conversations with people in other departments or see if you can schedule time with fellow interns. Explain that you want some exposure to other areas of the business. You might find something you like at another department, and you can request to work there the following summer or apply into the other department upon graduation. Even if you plan to apply outside of your current sphere at the end of the summer, keep working hard at your current position and don't seem ungrateful to your own boss.

Managing Big Buddies

Big buddies are good resources for getting acquainted with the company and potentially your new geographic location. They also can assist you with work questions. You can confide in them, and they are supposed to be confidential. However, if you have personality conflicts with anyone, you want to be diplomatic in what you share with your big buddy. He or she can provide advice, but you ultimately want to make sure that he or she gets a good impression of you. Your boss may solicit your buddy for his or her opinion about you during your final appraisal. Make a friend, but keep the relationship professional. He or she may not be active about keeping in touch with you. So, during your first meeting, you should ask the same as you did your boss in terms of setting up weekly or biweekly lunch meetings or coffee breaks. In this way, you keep your buddy (and yourself because you are forced to articulate how you are doing) up to date on your summer experience.

CHAPTER 12
A Few Work Tools for Tracking Your Performance

You should keep the lines of communication open with your boss by checking in with him/her frequently about your progress. The weekly or biweekly one-on-one session is an appropriate time to do this. If for some reason you do not see your boss often (because he may be away on travel or working from home), an email every now and then is in order. A work journal is a great way to help organize your thoughts. This is an exercise that you would perform most frequently. The project log and 5/15 reports are just a couple samples of how you can present your work summary in an organized fashion.

Work Journals

Keeping a journal about your work experience can be beneficial to you when it comes time for your performance appraisal, to prepare for interviews, or to update your resume. It also helps you to keep tabs on how you like your job and if it measures up to your expectations. For me, it reminded me that I had a productive day after all. Sometimes, I felt like I just sat around at my cubicle for hours on end without accomplishing anything. Some of my intern friends would count the money they made as the hand of a clock moved around. However, I like being productive, and keeping a journal forced me to think about what I accomplished at work each day.

Indeed, keeping a journal takes lots of discipline. You should keep one if you find it helpful. Perhaps, a weekly recap is enough for your purposes. I tried a daily system, which didn't stick for my second internship but surprisingly did on my third internship.

The Project Log

I have included in the Appendix an example of this. It summarizes the name of my project, the project owner, hours I contributed toward the project each month (some hours are forecasted), and a summary of accomplishments following the CAR (context, action, results) method.

5/15 Reports

The report is named five-fifteen because it is meant to take no more than five minutes to read and no more than 15 minutes to write. The three key elements of the report are "What You've Done," "What You Plan To Do," and "Your Morale: How Are You Feeling About What You've Done or Plan To Do?" You can answer these three questions in paragraph form (one paragraph per section), or in bullet/list format. An online search for 5/15 will reveal that some variations to the three sections exist, but the system I present here has worked well for me.

CHAPTER 13
Surprises

Performance in the Eye of the Beholder

Performance evaluations are ironic. They are meant to be objective (often, based on a numeric scale). However, they are extremely subjective.

At UPS, my manager asked me to rank my own performance according to a list of metrics. On a scale of 1 to 5 (3 as average, and 5 as excellent), I remember giving myself several 4's and occasionally some 3's and 5's. I thought I did a very a satisfactory job that summer for an intern. My manager evaluated me differently. He gave me many 3's and a few 2's and 4's. Why? He was evaluating me as if I were a full-time employee. He said employees usually don't receive high marks (5's) until they've been with the company 10 years. The 5-ranking indicates that you have mastered some skill and reached your potential in that particular area. It also probably means that you've shown a lot of improvement over time. Okay, that makes sense too. I can see it his way, but I found it a little unfair. Applying his logic, you probably deserved an A in third grade for a paper you wrote, but the teacher gives you a C because he reserves A's just for eighth-graders who are supposed to write super quality papers.

Here's the lesson from Internship 1: If you are asked to do a similar exercise like ranking yourself, you might want to clarify how you should approach it. Are you looking at the present? How did you do against some hypothetical standard for the work you did? Or, are you looking at the future? How did you do in relation to some future standard (a potential that's not achievable for you right now)?

At Merck, I had an even more devastating (now, comical) experience come evaluation time. I again was measured as if I were a full-time employee, but this time I really felt wronged. The evaluation asked my manager to provide examples of what I did well and where I could improve. I disagreed with her suggestions for improvement on two fronts: 1) she never expressed the concern to me previously and pretty much denied me a midway evaluation, and 2) her concerns seemed like unreasonable expectations for an intern. They were 1) I asked too many questions. I asked the Access guru in my group some questions about Access. I took only two to five minutes of his time each time to do so, and he did not seem bothered. My manager suggested that I call the help desk to resolve technical issues. This part I find outrageous (hence, comical) because the help desk puts you on hold for half an hour and often is unable to resolve your issue. 2) She was disappointed that I didn't think out of the box. Since when are interns supposed to think out of the box when we are trying to learn the ropes of what work is like? I wouldn't know how to do things differently before I really understand how things are done in the first place.

I suspect that she did not like me due to a personality clash. While I thought we were mature enough to separate personal matters from the business ones, this turned out not to be the case. However, I still learned a lot from the situation, and I identified my own list of areas for improvement. Here are the many lessons from Internship 2:

1) She was chatty; I was not. This is when I realized that I had been a workhorse all summer. No good.

2) Don't pass up that midway evaluation! We decided not to have one because she didn't give me my first project till a month into my summer. Two action items came out of this one:

    a. Ask for a three-quarters evaluation, so the final one isn't a surprise.

    b. See what you can do before your summer starts to make sure that an assignment welcomes your arrival. This is why I advocate doing the "pre-conversation" after you accept your offer and before you start work. This is a good idea for co-ops and entry-level positions too but is less critical because even if you do not get a project during the first month or two on the job, you should have ample time to work on it before your first evaluation.

A note to the Employer: There are a few things that an intern expects. Although it's not mandatory, it seems like basic etiquette that your summer boss should take you out to lunch during your last week as a thank you for the work that you did.

Taking your temporary hire out to lunch at the close of the internship or co-op really is just a nice gesture. My manager at Merck failed to do so. Another manager of equal status invited his intern to lunch and even extended the invitation to me. I do not remember why I declined the offer. However, I left that internship devastated. That was the last straw. Before I could think about the situation objectively and arrive at the above action items, I had to dig myself out of depression. Indeed, the whole experience had a serious effect on me. I am thankful for my parents and career counselor for helping me come to terms, and I now fully appreciate the experience. Who knows? Perhaps, my manager would give me the same, silly evaluation even if I had done things differently. However, at least I would know with full certainty that the problem really was hers. I felt at ease just knowing that I had some control over my fate and that I could apply some lessons to minimize future devastation.

At SBC, everything went right! My manager was great, but I shall take some credit. I initiated a pre-conversation. He gave me his expectations at the start of the summer. I wasn't a workhorse. I asked insightful questions that helped him to clarify my project. I had an interesting assignment, and I was given a great deal of responsibility, which I had learned not to expect as an intern. I had a midway evaluation, and I received a stellar final evaluation. The SBC scale goes from "does not meet", "meets", to "exceeds" expectations. I received the third mark. He treated me to lunch during my last week. I could not have asked for a better summer experience.

Academia vs. Real World

I had quite a reality check in store for me when I first started working. I was used to solving textbook problems and flipping to the end of the book to check if my answers were correct. Work, for the most part, is nothing like that. You do the best with what you've got. I did some data analysis on rather imperfect data. Unfortunately, you learn to deal. You will be shocked at the inefficiencies that you come across in business, but you may have opportunities to change it for the better. Don't lose hope. For right now, accept it as it is, and don't let it get to you. I did, and I was so disappointed. However, this was one of the more valuable lessons I learned from industry. That's why work experience is so important. It puts your studies in perspective. You are getting an undergraduate degree to learn how to think and solve problems. In industry, many more than one way exists to solve a problem, and often the problems are not even defined for you, and they almost never involve a textbook.

Dealing with Ambiguity

Take the bull by its horns. If you are running into a wall because you are unclear about what you are supposed to do, you should ask your boss or colleague for more direction. However, sometimes, your boss may not have the answer, as was the case in my third internship. I was told to draft up an executive summary of how an organization should be redesigned. What did my boss mean by "executive summary" and to what organization redesigns was he referring? Actually, I had to come up with the recommendations first on how to redesign the organization, and then I would be able to draft the document. After cursing my boss for a good half a day for taking the Friday off before the Monday deadline he had given me, I began my brainstorming efforts. I started by looking at the current organization and jotted down what he disliked about it. I outlined the process and related the process to a manufacturing environment. What was the "bottleneck" step that held up the process? Was he concerned with this and/or the return on investment he mentioned? What about the lack of communication between the several parties involved in the group? Was he also concerned about accountability? I raised all these questions to him on Monday instead of presenting him with a draft executive summary, and he was incredibly impressed. I was able to crank out the executive summary by Tuesday with the new direction. The trick to dealing with ambiguity is to ask the right questions. If you ask your boss or colleague an open-ended question on what he means by so and so, he or she may respond ambiguously. If you have more specific questions prepared after you've arrived at your three best guesses, he or she can verify if you are on track or not.

Feeling Bored and Asking for More Work

Chances are you will feel bored at some point during your first job. If you conduct a good pre-conversation with your boss and make sure that a project awaits you when you arrive on the job, you will decrease your chances of feeling bored. However, even if you have a project, you probably could handle multiple projects or you may be working with others on your one. When other people are involved, you may not be able to proceed with a project because you are waiting on someone else to give you information. In these circumstances, first try calling the person you are waiting for to see how you can help him/her get you what you need and use the phone call (not email) as a friendly reminder. Full-time employees can get hundreds of emails a day, so yours can be easily missed inadvertently.

Once you've done as much as you can with your project or projects and the balls are in other people's courts, try seeking out other work for yourself. You can look for computer-based training, organize your files and document what you've learned so far, or do some socializing or informational interviews. You can approach your colleagues as well to see how you can alleviate some of their workloads. The last thing you want to do is complain to your boss about feeling bored even if s/he didn't do his/her part in giving you enough work. If you have tried everything else and the boredom persists for several days, you should approach your boss. However, do not go empty handed! Go to him/her with some ideas on what else you'd like to do (either some items you come up with by yourself or areas you'd like exposure to guide your boss in finding work that's suitable to you). Usually, building on a current project is a good bet. You can grow the scope of your project if you see other opportunities for improvement that weren't outlined for you to address already.

I understand that coming up with work for yourself and identifying your interests is particularly challenging when you have little experience because you don't know what you don't know. The best way to resolve this conflict is to mingle. Learn about what others do. Ask other interns, your colleagues, or your assigned buddy about what they do to get a sense for what else is out there beyond your own work.

Making a Project Truly Yours

Sometimes, you experience boredom because your project is ill defined. You cannot return it to your boss though. If it is "broke", YOU must fix it. Brainstorm how you can make the project more complicated somehow. By the way, this will win you wowing points because it shows great initiative. For example, during my first internship, I was presented with a forecasting project. The forecasting method was not anything fancy and was a simple scaling down of national forecasts issued by headquarters. Headquarters also dictated that the accuracy should fall within two percent above or below the forecasts. Unfortunately, the forecasting method was not very good, and my forecasts were grossly inaccurate.

Nobody was to blame, but I was frustrated that my forecasts were useless and that reflected poorly on me. I began doing my research and trying a new forecasting method based off local records. In the end, I recommended that the district collect local data for the sake of more accurate forecasts. I wish I had done this a month into my internship when I was bored out of mind at the tediousness of the task. I waited till the week before my summer ended, so I do not know what came of my recommendations. If I had come up with this project expansion a month earlier, I may have been able to scrap my inaccurate forecasting in favor of taking the project yet a step further by defining a process by which to collect the data necessary to make accurate forecasts.

The Biggest Adjustment

All of the above considered, perhaps the worst thing about work life is waking up and going to sleep early or giving into coffee. I never could handle coffee, so I had to rely on getting enough sleep. Waking up at 7am is tough, and you are pretty exhausted by the end of the day to do much else other than eat dinner, take a nap, or watch television. I picked up some pleasure reading and reconnected with old friends to pass the other time. Getting a gym pass or exercising would have been a wise move as well, and I would encourage you to look into how you spend your time outside of work. If you do not take the time to make your non-work life enjoyable, you will feel like all you do for a living is make a living. You do the math: you most likely work at least eight hours, get an additional hour for lunch and breaks, and you spend an additional hour or two getting ready, winding down, and commuting to and from work. Those work activities total to about 11 hours and if you sleep for eight, you have only five hours left for yourself. Plan and use that time wisely. Hey! At least, you don't need to worry about homework or studying on your evenings and weekends!

If you are not working at home, you should consider a car. I somehow thrived without one, but I really wish I had one when I needed to get groceries or if I wanted to meet a friend a few cities away.

PART 5
REFLECTING ON YOUR EXPERIENCE

CHAPTER 14
Making the Most out of Your Experience

You Are Your Best Teacher

Congratulations on making it this far! What are your impressions of the work you did, the company's culture, your department, your relationship with your colleagues and your boss? Do you want to return to this company next year? If yes, do you want to return to this same department or try something new? How did your performance appraisal compare with how you thought you did? What aspects of the internship did not meet your expectations? What will you do differently next time in anticipation of potential outcomes that you disliked? For example, I pursued the following improvements:

- Thinking more carefully about my start date so that I would not miss the formal welcoming from my department and lose out getting to know other interns before they formed a clique.
- Initiating a pre-conversation to make sure a project welcomed me upon arrival and to lay down expectations for a successful term.
- Learning to be more of a social butterfly and to be more proactive on the job.

You will develop your own list of what you can do better next time with some thorough analysis and engagement of your emotional response to the internship experience. If you are in full swing at an entry-level position, you should take some time off from work every few months to reflect on your experience. I'd encourage to you to go out of town for a few days to get a fresh perspective on how you can improve as you continue working.

Asking for a Letter of Reference

If you decide at the end of your summer or co-op or a few years into your entry-level position that you might want to pursue a graduate degree, then consider asking your current or former supervisor whether he or she would be willing to write you a letter of reference. Although I have not looked into graduate school, I asked one of my former bosses to submit a letter on my behalf for some undergraduate scholarship applications.

You should ask for this letter only if you believe you made a good impression and if you think he or she would be agreeable to serving as your reference. Sometimes, your managers may feel funny about serving as your reference if you do not return or plan to work for them the following year because they do not extend you an offer or you decide to go elsewhere and have communicated this. Also, keep in mind that although many will be agreeable to helping you with your education (scholarships or admittance into graduate school), asking them to serve as a job reference may be asking too much for the reason that they feel funny.

What to Do If You Left on Not So Good Terms?

First and foremost, never badmouth your boss. If you are asked why you decided not to return to a particular company, answer honestly but you can leave your boss out of the response. My bosses played a huge role in my satisfaction (or dissatisfaction) with each of my internships. However, I explained during my interview for my third internship that I did not feel challenged in my previous internships. In the first case, I did not learn very much. My work was rather repetitive. So, while my project lasted two-months, the bulk of my learning ended in two weeks. In my second case, I did not get my project until a month into my internship. I asked for more work and only got small day assignments for the first month. While fellow interns completed four projects by the summer's end, I had done only two. I felt that my first month was not very well spent.

If you are asked to list your manager's name and contact information, you can be assured that most companies will call just to confirm that you actually worked there. What I usually do is write my manager's name and provide the general contact information for the company (for instance, your human resource contact). This way, the next company has enough information to verify that you did indeed work where you said you worked. Be sure to list professors, advisors, mentors, or even well respected peers as your reference. Unless they say so, you are not obliged to list your previous boss. If you've made friends at your old workplace with other managers or senior people, you can ask them if it is okay to list them as a reference too without providing details about your clash with your boss.

Did It Feel Like a Waste of Time?

I felt like some of my internships were a waste of time in the sense that I did not pickup many technical skills. However, companies actually may think otherwise. Many of my interviewers were impressed that I was exposed to business problems that their companies also face, and they were highly interested in how my former employers resolved the problem. If you do not know how to phrase your project so that it sounds impressive, visit your career center or ask a mentor or friend who successfully survived a job hunt before you. Most importantly, be confident during your interview. Do not underestimate your internship. Even if you did not find the work interesting, at least now you know what you do not like or what you need to do to make it more interesting the next time.

How to Leverage Your Experience for Future Work

Every experience is valuable whether you think so or not! Don't settle or sell yourself short. You are in a great position once you have at least one internship under your belt, not just because work experience speaks louder than all else on your resume but also because you are more familiar with what you like and what you want from your career.

After my third summer internship with SBC, I really wanted to return there for full-time work. When I mentioned this to my mentors, they all asked if I was sure that was what I wanted to do. I justified in my mind why, but I of course had doubts if that was the best direction for me. I ended up interviewing dozens more companies and landed five other offers. This company ended up in third place. I took two weeks to break the tie between the top two choices, but this was a great exercise for me, and I continued to sharpen my mingling skills. I've noticed how I've grown more polished, extroverted, and better connected every time I survive a job hunt.

PART 6
TABLES TURNED

CHAPTER 15
The Case Study of Fran

I have a few final thoughts as seen through my entry-level eyes. I also want to offer a few additional comments on the internship experience through observing another summer intern at my current organization at Procter & Gamble. I will refer to this intern as Fran.

Work Priorities (Internship Committees vs. Real Work)

Some of the more structured internships offer opportunities for you to develop leadership skills through company-sponsored "extra-curricular" commitments. I served on the College Night committee at Merck and as Community Service Chair at SBC. College Night was an event, where interns showcased their school to high school-aged children of employees. The committee was a lot of fun because I got to know some more interns that way. The Community Service position was less involved because the SBC program I was part of was rather small (just eight), so my responsibility was to organize one activity for the group.

All eight interns in my program had a position, and we received communication upfront that work takes priority. The College Night Committee did not communicate this, nor did the committee at P&G communicate this to the intern in my group. The result of this was that Fran spent a lopsided amount of time on this "extra-curricular" activity, and the leaders within my group questioned the value of this committee. I believe this is the primary reason why she did not receive an offer. As one of my colleagues put it, although she performed superbly on that committee, she failed to impress with regard to the real work she was assigned. She would have been much better off doing a mediocre job for the committee and performing superbly at her work.

I would encourage you to participate in these "extra-curricular" activities only if you can handle it on top of your daily work. Remember that your involvement in such activities will provide only bonus points at best during the hiring decision. However, the intangible value is that you may build great friendships and gain other leadership experience from that involvement.

Confidence at Work

Exuding confidence is highly important once you arrive at the job.

Remember that you likely could credit your offer with this one quality! I shared a project with Fran. We had to interview an expert within the company about our project's subject. During this interview, she often preceded her questions with "Can I ask?" The better approach would be to ask directly. Asking permission when you get the signal that time is running short is appropriate. However, asking permission to ask a question, especially when the setting already dictates you have a right to ask, leaves a bad impression. She seemed to lack confidence or simply a sense of appropriate behavior.

Are You the Right Fit?

Have you ever heard or used this line about a professor? "S/he is nice but can't teach." You like the professor great as a person because s/he is very personable and approachable. However, although the intent is there, s/he is not very helpful when it comes to helping you learn. Do you find that you actually seem to respect more the professor who is a jerk but is a great instructor? When you were asked to evaluate your instructor, you probably gave both style professors at least average marks because you appreciated the efforts of the first and the quality of the work in the latter.

To be in the best position, you need to meet both criteria of being personable and doing a good job at what the employer expects of you just as you expect from your professors to be good at teaching.

No one could argue with the statement that Fran was very sweet. Unfortunately, she fell short in the other dimension. Her work was okay, but her work style did not lend itself well to the needs of our group. As a colleague put it, she works very hard and could be a superstar in another organization, but she lacks some of the initiative and self-directedness which are desirable, if not imperative, to survive in our group.

You should take time to learn and observe what's valued in your group and do your own assessment of how well you fit. Many of my skills are learned, so you too can be proactive about trying to fit your function's style. This does not mean you need to compromise your values, but you do need to seem assimilated.

Time Management

Get your work done in the time allotted to you! If you feel that your workload is too heavy, you need to say so and ask for help. However, I bet your workload is totally manageable if not too light. So, get your work done! If you need to write a list to help manage your time, do so religiously. I am a big fan of lists, but I usually keep a mental to-do list in my head. You should not show signs that you cannot handle the work because the expectation is that you will have more work when you are full-time, entry-level. If you cannot handle work as an intern, how are you going to handle more work as a full-time employee?

Fran made the mistake of suggesting that we meet over the weekend to do a project. I believe her when she said that she was in school mode when often the only time you can meet to do a team project is on the weekend, and our boss seemed to understand. Unfortunately, little slips do add up. Sometimes, I wish companies were more understanding that you have little experience in the real world, which contributes to some of your imperfect behavior. However, the reality is that the only measure that the employer can make is what s/he observes from your summer. For me, the third time (both company and internship) was the charm.

<u>Eating Lunch Alone</u>

Eating at your desk on a regular basis can be problematic if you are an intern because it implies that you are anti-social or that you have trouble managing your time. Although you may not embody any of these qualities, you are giving that impression. I must say that my full-time organization is the most inviting of any I've seen. Whenever any of us is hungry, we walk around to see who else is ready for lunch. We always made sure to invite Fran too even though she sat in the next row of cubes and could have been overlooked by accident.

I hardly ever ate lunch with my boss during my internships. However, I usually had a good base of intern friends to call on for lunch. Ideally, you should strike a balance between eating lunch with your group members and the other interns or any other friends you make within the company.

Also, note that taking lunch actually improves your productivity. Do not follow the bad example that some full-time employees set by eating at their desk. Unless they are exceptionally busy on a certain assignment, they give off the same bad impression of being anti-social or demonstrating poor time management. However, the employer probably did not have the benefit of prescreening these people over an internship, and some companies seem averse to dismissing people. Certainly, not eating lunch with your peers is not reason enough to lose your job. However, it certainly does not help your career. People want to know you as a person, not a robot who just churns out work. Remember to avoid the status of workhorse and social butterfly. Find the balance!

Be Cognizant of Who Makes the Hiring Decision

Be aware of who makes the hiring decision, and sell yourself accordingly. Fran had to give two summer presentations at the end of her internship (one for my group and the other for the internship program advisory committee). She used the presentation with us as her test run for the internship program, but she had mistaken the priorities again. My group was the one that makes the hiring decision. Her lack of preparedness in presenting to us reflected poorly. My group was a good sport in offering her plenty of constructive feedback in getting her ready for the one she deemed more important. I attended her second presentation, and it was much better. However, when I made this comment to her manager, he responded that there were still rough spots and that her hiring decision had been made after her first presentation.

CHAPTER 16
Final Remarks from an Entry-Level Perspective

Another Note on Start Dates

I feel very fortunate to have started work when I did. I had dreamt of an extravagant summer vacation to celebrate graduation from college. Indeed, many of my friends had great travels in Europe. However, in order to take advantage of my new company's old benefits plan that was due to change in July, I started at the end of June only five weeks after graduation. What I did not anticipate was that just as I was joining, the administrative assistant in my department was preparing to leave, and her role was being transitioned to three other administrative assistants outside my immediate group. I was lucky that our admin took good care of me in making sure I had a smooth transition into work. She setup my computer, requested supplies, and decorated my cubicle for me. At one of my summer internships, my security badge did not arrive until a month into my internship. So, I thought it was great that I did not need to sweat the little stuff. I can't imagine starting in September as originally planned because I do not know who would end up with the responsibility and have the time to get my basic needs together.

Glamour of Internships

Structured internship programs at big companies can be a lot of fun because the dynamic outside of work is like a summer camp. You meet new friends and attend company-sponsored professional and social events, which are often scheduled during work hours. The company also showers you with gifts and gives you access to senior level people. At SBC, the other corporate summer managers and I had the privilege of having breakfast with the CEO (Chief Executive Officer) of the western branch of the company and President of a main division. The closest my boss and my boss's boss ever came to meeting these people was shaking their hands. Take advantage of these unique opportunities because they expire once you become a full-time hire! Don't worry; there are plenty of other things that you can look forward to after your internship days.

If you don't work for a big and structured program, you'll never feel deceived by the disconnection between how interns are treated vs. new hires are treated. I encourage you to appreciate your internship because this is an exploratory time where mistakes are expected and won't be crippling to your career. This is also an opportunity for you to meet new people and hopefully, experience living in a new place.

What You Can Look Forward To

The internship can be stressful. People often say you'll definitely get the full-time job, but we all know that's not true. Thinking positively does help because it can reinforce positive behavior and a positive impression you leave with others. However, there is no guarantee. You have to get through the internship and usually another round of interviews or the final presentation. Both the interview and presentation require lots of preparation when you're not a natural. If you haven't interviewed since you landed the job, you are rusty already. So, be sure to brush up on the interview skills. Check the Appendix for tips on presentations.

What is tough about the internship is that you may fall in love with the company and not get an offer. Even if you don't love the place, you still want an offer because you feel vulnerable without one. You have doubts, like will you be able to land another job if this company doesn't want you back? In this situation, yes!! You just need to be proactive and follow the steps outlined in Part 2 of this book all over again. Although hearing rejection definitely is not easy, you may realize later that the decision was a blessing in disguise. Just give yourself some reflection time.

The beauty of full-time work is that you have passed—you have been accepted somewhere. There is less of a probationary feel to the work environment. You do need to continue to prove yourself and give a good impression or that may limit your growth potential, but that's not flat out rejection. I have found that working full-time to be much more meaningful and rewarding than internship projects because you are around long enough to see a project from start to finish. Intern projects are not usually self-contained, but a small piece of a large project. You get a better sense of how the puzzles fit together when your time at work does not expire abruptly after a few short months.

On top of gaining that sense of belonging and a better understanding of how things work, you can look forward to a pretty good life outside of work. I like exploring my new, more permanent residence. You will have an opportunity to do this too unless you move back in with your parents. The best part about most full-time positions is that you get your nights and weekends to spend any way that you want without worrying about homework or an upcoming quiz or test. You also have a steady flow of income, which tends to enable a better quality of life than when you were a poor college student.

EPILOGUE
Don't Forget to Enjoy the Ride

I found the job hunt a lot of fun because it was a great opportunity to meet new people, to travel to new cities, and to perfect the art of mingling and interviewing. Remember you learn as you go. So, do not expect to become an expert in this process overnight. However, I hope that by reading this book and using it as a reference, it will save you some stress in guessing what to do.

Quick Takeaways

1. Start NOW!
2. Try everything…many times!
3. Be proactive!
4. Be confident!
5. Go get your job!

Where to Go for More Information

I'd love to hear from you! Please visit www.hellorealworld.com, and let me know how your search went and your key learning or additional questions for me.

Also, be sure to take advantage of these additional resources:

News and Tips from me to you!

Message Board for college students to post burning questions, to share their experiences, and to dialogue with other students

Subscribe Page* to signup for exclusive quarterly newsletters

Additional Recommendations on where to go to learn more about job-enhancing topics (such as networking and career planning)

* "For the Student," "For the Employer", or "For the Mentor"

APPENDIX 1
Internships vs. Co-ops

If you have the flexibility to do a co-op (taking an entire semester or quarter off from school to go work, so the internship is extended from two months to three to six), I would look into it juxtaposed to studying abroad. I was intent on graduating on time, and I didn't want to overload myself during a particular semester in the interest of freeing up one for other purposes. So, although I have not done a co-op before, I do see value to a co-op.

I have a couple reasons. Reason 1) Two of my three internships weren't very interesting. I was bored because I either didn't get enough responsibility up front or I wasn't assigned enough projects to keep me busy. Some employers find it difficult to find meaningful work if you are there for only two months. According to that, your employer should have no problem finding you good work if you are there for six months.

Reason 2) Unfortunately, the corporate pace is typically much slower than the one you are accustomed to at school where there is a clear beginning and end to a term. Any project that you are assigned during an internship is probably just a small segment of a larger project that is worked on by several people. One of the most valuable aspects of an internship is to see the impact and communicate it in terms of dollars on your resume and for future interviews. For example, I saved Y dollars for Company ABC by streamlining process Z. When you are on the job for only two months, your contribution may be very significant, but you won't see the fruits of your labor before you leave. If you're on a project for six months, you will have a higher probability of seeing your impact. Of course, some projects span several years and even decades, but you should be able to measure the progress you make on the segment over which you had ownership.

If you don't see it before you run out of time, you can call up a friend within the company a few months later and inquire about the status of the project you were assigned and see how impactful your work was to it.

I would not recommend the following response to an interview question, but I used it a few times because I left my internship on somewhat sour terms with my supervisor, so I did not feel comfortable calling to see how my project went. I've been prompted during an interview to state the results of a certain project. I happened to receive this project three weeks before my internship was up, so I answered that I provided the analysis to the team, and they took it from there after I left. A better response would be to explain what the team did with my analysis after I left. For instance, my analysis enabled the team to derive a way to reduce the complete time for a standard procedure by Y hours.

To recap, if your schedule allows, a co-op is superior to an internship because you are more likely to get meaningful work and also more likely to see the fruits of your efforts. On the other hand, I do not regret going the internship route instead because two of my internships were rather imperfect in not measuring up to my high expectations. The two and half months each were plenty to get a bad taste and learn about my work behavior and likes and dislikes about work.

APPENDIX 2
Project Log

The project log helps you keep track of what you accomplished and hours spent on a particular project. Here's how I organized mine:

Project	Assisting	June	July	August	Accomplishments
Barceloneta ORSD Performance to Merial	Sam	7	0	0	This project sought to determine why a substantial gap existed between meeting shipments as promised and meeting shipments as requested. I performed the data analysis, which indicated little to no relationship between the accuracy of forecasts and delivering on time.
OE Savings Reporting	Susan	6	0	0	I made an excel version of the OE Savings tool in development.
Sterile/Non-sterile Routing (IMPACT)	Sarah	4	0	0	I audited IMPACT to verify that changes were made to the problematic workcenters.
Cognos Reports	Sam	15	0	0	I ran reports for the Standard Hours and Yield Trends to verify information was current for profit plan.
IMPACT Updates	Susan	10	0	0	I learned how to make basic changes in IMPACT and updated some run hours and move and queue times.
BWO Costing	Sarah	25	5	0	I verified information and sought clarifications on the Biological Work Order requests and then costed them accordingly.
Profit Plan	Sam	10	0	0	I made a model that compared last year's forecasted run times to the current year's and mapped the trends on a chart for centers: 160-Release prior to packaging and 236-Release prior to distribution. The charts indicated that workload was such that in heavy months the centers require overtime but in low months experience worker "starvation". The recommended hire policy would be to hire the average at the start of the year when workload tends to be heavier and let the attrition (vacancy) rate naturally level out the work/labor ratio.

APPENDIX 3
Recommended Courses

Organizational Behavior

I would recommend that you take a course on Organizational Behavior. This class gives you a sense of some theories behind how people perform at work and familiarizes you with self-assessment tools, such as Myers-Brig, and performance review processes, such as 360-degree feedback.

Corporate Finance

I think the concepts I use the most in work are what I learned from my course on Corporate Finance (also known as Engineering Economics). This course familiarizes you with common terms, such as NPV: Net Present Value and ROI: Return On Investment. Companies are interested in getting more out of what they put in, and these are standard measurements to track whether an investment paid off or not.

APPENDIX 4
Recommended Extra-curricular Activities

Building Your Resume

Please note that gaining experience should be your primary focus, not to look good on your resume. I have found that my peers that joined a student organization for its resume benefits missed the point. Being elected to a position with a title is not enough. If you want to have something to show and to talk about during an interview, you must fulfill the responsibilities of your position. Treat any volunteer position as if it were a real job. If you focus your attention on gaining experience, you will learn a great deal and have more than enough material for your resume and behavioral interviews. I actually ended up with too much, and I ran out of space on my one-page to cover all my experiences.

I have identified several skills, which I find particularly valuable in the working world and which can help immensely during your job search process. Start by joining only one or two organizations because you may overextend yourself if you try to tackle everything at once. You should look for positions that will allow you to develop multiple skills at once. I recommend joining an organization that you are interested in but taking on responsibility that puts you out of your comfort zone a little.

Learning Professionalism

Fundraising and corporate/industrial relations, a position where you organize a career fair or panel, are surprisingly similar to the job hunt process. In these roles, you are asking a professional for something (money, attendance at your event, or a job). In doing so, you must practice establishing a good impression and rapport with the professional and utilize strong writing and follow-up skills. In spite of your best efforts, you will encounter rejection. Thus, the number's game applies here too. The more professionals you approach, the more likely you will reach your goal of raising funds for your cause or securing a great lineup of companies for your career event. The bonus from volunteering for such a position besides learning a great deal is that you will be developing your own network, which can come in handy when you are looking for that internship, co-op, or entry-level position.

Demonstrating Leadership

Volunteering or running for an elected position with a title and subsequent responsibilities is a great way to demonstrate leadership. By fulfilling your responsibilities, you also set yourself up for asking the highest-ranking leader within that organization for a job reference down the line.

Sharpening Communication

Public speaking is a very helpful skill. I thought I would develop this by being involved in student government. One of my friends did improve his speaking skills a great deal from serving on student government, but this was not the case for me. I think my time would have been better spent in a debate club or theater group. I have found that my most articulate friends debated or acted in either high school or college. I wish I had done one of those instead. However, there are other means to the end. Some of your leadership positions require that you make announcements to your general membership about upcoming events or soliciting help. Also, you can look into Toastmasters International, which is an organization dedicated to helping you develop public speaking skills. The basic manual takes you through ten speeches.

Mingling

Organizations that offer regional and national conferences are a big bonus. I was involved in the Institute of Industrial Engineers, the Society of Women Engineers, and Golden Key International Honour Society—all offered conferences. I've attended several conferences run by each and enjoyed a great time at all of them. I already shared how some of them revealed the way to some job offers. Conferences provide other benefits besides a great mingling opportunity. You can volunteer to organize a conference as the chair of or serve on the organizing committee, which means you would be learning professionalism and demonstrating leadership. Typically, the organizing committee's job is also to welcome all the guests during the actual conference. Hence, there is a good chance that you can exercise your public speaking skills at that time too. Some conference programs also involve many workshops. If you feel knowledgeable on a topic and have something to share, you can volunteer to run a workshop—another great opportunity to sharpen your communication skills!

APPENDIX 5
Where to Find a Mentor

Mentors can come in any form. I have many older friends whom I view as mentors, but they see me simply as a friend. Most people are willing to help, but you need to ask them for it. However, I also find a lot of benefit to having official mentors. Many of my mentorship relationships naturally have developed into friendships.

There are several ways to find a mentor. Some student organizations offer a big buddy program to match up a junior or senior in your major to a freshman or sophomore. The Engineers Joint Council, an umbrella organization for all the engineering societies, did this on my campus. I would encourage you to participate as a big or little buddy. You also can look into your school's alumni association and see if they have a student-alumni program in place. Several professional organizations with student chapters also provide access to professional mentors. If you have a science or engineering background, you can signup for an e-mentor (a mentor-protégé relationship conducted over email) on MentorNet. If you still have trouble finding a formal program, I would encourage you to ask your professor, family members, or neighbors for suggestions. Perhaps, some of them would be willing to serve as your mentor too.

APPENDIX 6
Tips on Presentations

When you work on a project all summer, you are deeply familiar with it. However, think back to when you were first assigned the project. Did you immediately understand the problem's scope and how to approach it? No! You probably received a good description and asked clarifying questions before you dove into your assignment and as you made progress on it. Presentations are tricky because you are allotted only 10-20 minutes to summarize the work you did over a few months. Due to your limited time, you need to simplify your summary down to the bare essentials. Also, if your work is fairly technical or uses many acronyms, be sure you dumb down your presentation and spell out terms unique to your work and immediate organization because you should not expect your audience to be familiar with the context of your work.

Simplify the Message

The best way to present your work is to follow the popular behavioral interview style, CAR: Context, Action, and Result. Provide background for your project and the purpose in how it relates to improving the business. Then, explain how you went about addressing the problem. Conclude with the recommendations you made and its impact on the company's financial situation, productivity, or other concern. When possible, quantify the exact dollar savings or timesaving you expect to generate once your recommendations are implemented. You can work with your supervisor or team members on calculating this number. Explain that you want to tag a value to the work you performed over the summer and that you could use some guidance in calculating that number.

Simplify the Visual Aid

When designing the power point presentation, keep it simple. Aim to spend one minute per slide, but do not overload the slide with words. Begin with a descriptive title, a topic sentence, and provide a few supporting bullet points. When appropriate, put in pictures to support the message in your slide or ideas you are trying to convey in your presentation. Visit www.hellorealworld.com for examples of presentations.

Organize the Content

The following is the typical format of an end-of-summer presentation:

Title Page

Presentation Agenda

Introduction To You (introduce yourself in terms of where you go to school, your class level, and your major)

Introduction To Your Organization (very brief description of your organization's purpose within the business)

Project 1 (use CAR)

Project 2 (use CAR)

Project 3 (use CAR)

Summary of Accomplishments

Lessons Learned

Suggestions To Internship Committee (what could they do better for next time? Keep it diplomatic).

Acknowledgements (thank your boss, buddy, and anyone else who helped you during the internship)

Plan Ahead

I loved my last summer internship so much that I really wanted to make a strong impression for my presentation. I spent nearly 20 hours on the power point two weeks prior to my scheduled presentation date. I finalized the presentation the week before and did several practice runs with some friends to get feedback. My presentation received very high remarks on most fronts. However, I unintentionally offended some people by trying to be funny. You should be careful about using humor because it may be misinterpreted. Feedback upfront is helpful in making sure people get the message you are trying to deliver. The three things to keep in mind for the presentation are to keep it simple, be prepared, and keep it positive. You want to set a tone that you really enjoyed your experience and that you would love to return. Employers want to see how you were successful because that suggests you would be successful as a full-time employee.

Polish the Delivery

Practice your speech and make sure it is delivered within the allotted time. Resist the temptation to read off your presentation. The slides are there only as an outline for you. If you have 10 minutes, I would suggest spending no more than two minutes on the background of the presentation, yourself, and the organization. Spend the bulk of your time (five minutes) on explaining your projects. In the remaining three minutes, close your talk by highlighting your key accomplishments, lessons learned, and the people who contributed to your success. At the end of your presentation, you can invite questions.

I'm sure you've heard that you want to tell them what you will tell them, tell them, and then tell them again. Begin with the agenda of your speech. Tell them that you will be introducing yourself and your organization, provide a summary of your work, and conclude with some takeaways. Proceed with introductions. When you start talking about your projects, you may want to tell them that you are going to share three projects with them. Then start with the first. As you continue with the speech, use good transition phrases to cue the audience that you are moving to the next point. For example, you can say something as simple as "For my second project, I was asked to..."

Rest up and Dress up for Delivery Day

Try to get a good night's rest before your presentation day. Dress the part. Look sharp and professional. Dress more formally than you do usually. A full suit is not necessary unless mandated, but try to be on the formal-side of business casual if that's your company's regular dress policy. Perhaps, practice once more the day of the event so your ideas are fresh in your head, and just take a few deep breathes prior to the delivery.

J ENGYEE LIANG was born and raised in Orange County, California. She graduated from Marina High School in Huntington Beach in 2001 and earned a bachelor of science in industrial engineering & operations research from the University of California, Berkeley in 2005. Liang enjoys swimming, hiking, writing, traveling, and experiencing new places, including living in Cincinnati for her most recent job.